Learn to Love Yourself Again: 6 Steps to Self-Love

By Kayla Turnipseed

Remember to always love yourself!

♡, [illegible]

Printed by Createspace

Created and published through Kayla Turnipseed

Printed in the United States of America

Dedication

This book is dedicated to anyone that is struggling with loving themselves. Who is always second guessing themselves because they don't know what is right or wrong in the world. And those who want to make a difference but don't know where to begin.

Acknowledgements

I want to acknowledge my mom for always believing in me and setting an example of what it means to stand in your power.

My boyfriend, who encourages me to voice my opinions and to not be afraid of judgment from others.

Ascension Leadership Academy and Grace for helping me to find my voice and use it.

And to all the beautiful women that helped provide me with quotes for my book. Without their strong stand for self-love I probably wouldn't have written this book.

Introduction

"Love is the bridge between you and everything" ~ *Rumi*

Have you ever wondered why other people are happy? Why do people live an extraordinary life on little to no money? Why people are happy with their lives, rather than be sad, jealous or angry? It's because most people are generally happy and have self-love. Self-love is loving yourself for who you are, loving your strengths and weaknesses, and embracing them both.

Now, I know what you're thinking: *how could somebody be so happy loving themselves, being happy, and all that jazz?* Well, people work on themselves by going through personal development classes, they make changes to their normal schedule and they embrace just living their lives the way they want to. Whether you're happy with your current situation or you wish there could be more to your life, you can choose to be happy and see where that leads you.

I know many of you are thinking: *Well, how can I be happy when I'm utterly and truly just sad all the time and life doesn't seem to be working in my favor? When life seems to be throwing me in a tailspin and making me uncomfortable and unhappy?*

Well, this is what I'm here to tell you, to help share my story of finding self-love, and how I was able to overcome those fears. Do those negative feelings still creep up? You bet they do! But, you know what? I have learned through hard work and trusting in myself that I have a voice and I am seen.

Facing the truth about yourself is always going to be hard. But I am here to tell you that it's okay to be afraid and it's okay to be different. Our differences are what make us who we are. The people you feel as though you don't fit in with are probably not meant to be in your life to begin with—or only for a short period of time. If your friends aren't uplifting you, then you probably need new friends. There comes a time when you have to do what's right for you and only you.

In this book, I am here to show you how to make your life the best it can be when you stop and take care of yourself. By sharing my experience with you, I'm letting you know that you're not alone. Being alone makes you sad. Being alone makes you feel like the world is crashing in on you and you can't do anything to get yourself out of it. And yet, I am here to tell you that no matter what happens in your life, no matter how you feel, or what others say about you, you are never alone. Someone has gone through a similar journey that you are going through. Whether it is the exact same experience or not, everyone has their own story to tell.

Your story is unique. Your story is what makes you "you". Your story is what makes you happy and it's what you can look back on to tell people what you overcome to be where you are now. I have gone through a couple of trainings so far and have learned a lot about myself that I didn't realize before. I am in a good place and I have Ascension Leadership Academy to thank for that. I would never be happy with my current situation if I had not gone through that rigorous trainings and transformations to help me get out of my head, let go of my ego, and ultimately help me figure out who I truly am and who I truly can be. I still have many areas to work on in my life, but I have time and I am living in the now rather than in the past.

I would not have completed any of those trainings without facing my story and owning it. If we cannot own story or face our truth, how are we going to function in a society that is constantly changing? We can live our lives ignoring what happened in our past or we can own it and not let it control or future. When it comes to transformation, how are we showing up in the world around us? Are we making this a better place for everyone around us or are we in it for ourselves? Self-love and self-care play a pivotal role in how we treat others around us. If we cannot love ourselves, then we cannot truly love others. I hope through this book that you are able practice self-love and self-care to make a better life.

CONTENTS

Chapter 1

How to Block Negative Feedback

> she overcame everything
> that was meant to destroy her
> — sylvester mcnutt

Do you often feel jealous or feel unhappy in your current situation because someone else is living the life that you want to live? Do you struggle with unhappiness or jealousy every day of your life because you don't know how to be happy? Do you wonder why it is that others can be happy and you cannot? If you've answered "yes" to all of those questions, then you are in the right place. If we're being honest here, it really boils down to how people take what is negative and turn it into positive, turning it into something that is their own and that truly makes them happy.

To begin, you have to find compassion in your heart to love yourself. Self-love plays a major role in how we live our day-to-day life. It all starts with how we look at ourselves every morning and when we go to bed. If we wake up seeing only the flaws, then that is all we are going to see. We have the right to choose how we want our thoughts to be every time we wake up and start our day.

We live in a society where we are taught to have a perfect body or to look a certain way. Yet being different and outside of social norms are viewed as wrong, and can have a big impact on our own thoughts.

Negative thoughts do not come from out of the blue. They are caused by something traumatic that happened when we were growing up and followed us into teenage years or, in some cases, adulthood. It is those experiences that we hold on to because they either kept us grounded or take us on a downward spiral into self-hate.

I have seen so many people struggle with their negative thoughts that they eventually became a shell of the person that they once were. We are taught at a young age that it is okay for us to be ourselves and to be happy with who we are. Yet, somewhere along the lines, we either get bullied for being ourselves or we start to pretend to be someone else in order to be liked by other around us. This takes us away from being our true selves. We are allowing negativity to take over who we are as a person. We are not making space to allow us to be who we truly are.

"A man cannot be comfortable without his own approval."
– Mark Twain

I have struggled with self-image for a long time. I always thought I looked fat. I didn't look as fit as the other girls. I wasn't athletic. I wasn't happy in my own skin: *"I could go for bigger boobs. I feel like I'd be more attractive that way. And now if I got a little tummy tuck, I'd be happier."* But the truth is, deep down, I would be dying inside. All those "imperfections" that I have are what make me who I am and my negative voice took that power away from me.

You are you. You are unique. You are different. You are special in your own unique way. Half of the time, they're just jealous of you because you can hold your head high. You can be happy with who you are, what you bring to the table, and what you bring to the world. People are scared of that, so they want to bring you down their level, instead of raising you up.

For example, my sister she was always mean to me. She

always told me that I wasn't smart, that I was stupid, that I would never amount to anything, and that I was ugly. Those were the things that stood out to me more than anything than I have ever experienced growing up. It followed me well into adulthood and stayed throughout all of my relationships. I would purposefully sabotage my relationships because I could not be myself. I would pretend to be someone else for them to like me while holding back who I was until the relationship was over.

Negative feedback was something that I gave myself every day because I did not know what was possible in being positive. Positive emotions meant that I had to be myself and like who I was as a person. I would pretend every day that I would be happy so that others wouldn't ask me how I was—or, even get close to me. Negativity helped me to be someone else so I could survive the outside world. I was distancing myself from my loved ones.

Going through personal development trainings opened my mind up to the possibilities around me. It only took one weekend out of a five-weekend personal development training to help open my eyes up to the possibilities of self-love. I would beat myself up internally about what I did wrong or why I didn't look the way I wanted to. It took facing what I was hiding from everyone and myself to get to the point that I could be happy.

Throughout this narrative, you are probably wondering how this will help to block negative feedback. The truth is you can never truly block it. It will always there, but here are some ways to suppress the negative emotions and feedback as they come.

1) Acknowledge negative emotions/feedback as they pop up by listening to what they are saying. If that is not the way you want to feel, then voice your true feelings.

2) Find the root of where these negative feelings are coming from. Are they from your distant past? Something that happened recently? What happened in your life for these feelings to manifest themselves?

3) Look in the mirror and voice those negative thoughts. If they hurt or make it so you cannot look yourself in the eye, say something positive about yourself. Can you feel the shift in energy it has produced? Do you feel the power that positivity has on you?

4) Say *"I love you"* every day in the mirror to yourself even when negative thoughts arise. How does that make you feel? Do you automatically smile when you say it or do you show no emotion?

We all carry around baggage that is constantly keeping bringing us down. We are human and that is what we do. However, we do not always have to be like that. We can live our lives the way we want to. In truth, we can live without being afraid to be ourselves. When it really comes down to it, you hold the power to either make your feelings positive or negative. No one can take that away from you.

There is nothing that is wrong with you. *Let me repeat that again.* There is nothing that is wrong with you. You are who you are because you are who you are meant to me. Are you different than the rest? Yes. Are there things that you might want to change? Yes. Are you going to act on those changes? No. You get to choose your outlook on your life. You get to choose if you want to stay negative or if you want to be positive. The choice is always yours and you should never have to be afraid to be yourself.

On the next page, there are some questions to answer to get in the mindset of what is to come.

Remember, keep staying positive. It's contagious.

Question & Answer

What is your first memory of self-hate? How big of an impact did that have on your life?

If you could get rid of 1 negative thought, what would it be?

How could incorporating positive thoughts impact/change your mindset?

What is something you can do today to be a step closer towards living your dream life?

Chapter 2

The Meaning of Self-love

"Self-love begins with loving yourself fully just as you are in this moment here and now
. Fall in love with your freckles, wrinkles, and all the beautiful imperfections that make you exactly who you are! You are perfectly imperfect so just always remember to open your heart wide, love hard and love so much it hurts because that is where the most authentic side of you lives"

~Jill Smart RN, BSN, CTC
Soul Healing Practitioner and Founder of InHeartFlow

What does self-love mean to you? Is it a negative meaning or is it positive? Many people tend to go on the negative side when it comes to self-love. They think that anyone who practices self-love or self-care are selfish and don't care about others. I am guilty of thinking that way. When my mom would go out and get manicures, I thought that she didn't love my sister and I anymore. To me, this meant that she would rather be by herself than to be with her kids. It wasn't until I was older that I started to understand what self-care and self-love actually meant.

You can find a lot of videos on Facebook or Instagram showing people who have overcome negative thoughts from themselves and others around them. They learned to love themselves yet most of them have not given a meaning of what self-love is. My curious mind led me to the Merriam-Webster Dictionary of what self-love means. It says self-love means *"excessive regard for oneself, one's own interest, etc."* However, there are many meanings to self-love.

On my journey to self-love, there was a time when I did not understand what self-love truly meant. I thought it was being selfish and disregarding others for yourself in a negative way. I started to ignore my needs for someone else's because I wanted to please everyone around me. Through transformation, I was able to find out the person I neglected and started my journey of loving and caring for myself. I did not know that my journey to self-love would help me understand what love truly meant.

Self-love means many different things to everyone. It does not mean that you're selfish and only looking out for yourself. It means you care enough about yourself to hold love in your heart for others.

Taking time out for yourself does not mean that you don't care about anyone around you. It means that you need to let your body and mind recharge in a way that makes you happy. Some people might call you selfish or you might lose friends in the process. But whatever happens, it is never your fault for wanting to take the time out of your day love yourself. Your happiness is what matters most in the world to you and you need to make sure that you are happy.

I have struggled with self-image problems all of my life. I always thought that in order for me to be happy, I needed to change things about my physical body for someone to even notice me. I thought by doing so, people would like me or want to be like me. The image I had about myself was not the same image that everyone else saw. They saw someone that was strong, confident, and secure in their skin. And yet, I saw the opposite. It wasn't until I looked further in myself that I started to see who everyone else saw. And my meaning of self-love took a turn for the better. I started to take care of myself and be positive in the way I look at myself and feel about myself.

"For you to love anybody, including yourself, you have to have respect for them" ~ Diogenes Berroa

---

Self-love means you get to let somebody else love you, while also loving yourself. It doesn't care about what other people say, it doesn't matter what the media says about you, how you should look, or how you should be. Those don't matter. You get to be who you are. You get to be your unique self.

What makes you "you" is what you bring to the table. For example, I love to write and I love to read, and those are what make me "me". My ideal day would be having a glass of wine, cuddling up with my kitten, and reading a book. Taking a couple of hours out of your day to care for yourself can be the best hours of your life. They are the time you get to be an uninhibited "you". Your body is a temple and you need to treat it the way it is meant to be treated—with love, care, and respect.

I know a lot of people who would rather care for others before they care about themselves, and they wonder why they're not happy. The truth is, they're not happy because they're too busy taking care of others that they neglect to take care of themselves. So, I am giving you permission to take an hour out of your day for yourself, to take two hours, to take six hours out of your day to care for you. At the end of the day, all you have is you and what you bring to the table.

So, what is the meaning of self-love? Self-love means taking care of you, taking care of your body, learning to love your body. Learn to just take the time out of the day and be selfish. Take the time. Get a mani-pedi. Get your hair cut. Get your nails done. Do what makes you happy, because there is only a limited amount of time we have on this earth. There are a lot of people that live to be 105 without any regrets. They lived to be 105 because they took care of themselves and lived their lives the way they wanted to live it. They took care of who they were. At the end of the day, all you have is you. You go home to you. You look in the mirror at you. And when you die, you die with you. So it's best to live life now. Do the things that make you happy. Do the things that make you celebrate life and joy and make you super happy. Take the time for self-care and let it mean something to you.

Before we go to the next chapter, let's delve into the meaning of self-love more on the next page.

Question & Answer

What does self-love mean to you?

How does a life of self-love look for you?

Chapter 3

Practicing Self-Care

> "TO FALL IN LOVE WITH YOURSELF IS THE FIRST SECRET TO HAPPINESS."
>
> - ROBERT MORLEY

Was there a time in your life where you just wanted to have time for yourself? Time to do the things that you loved doing? And then life got in the way. You started new relationships, lost old ones that weren't serving you and your needs got lost in all the chaos. Your view of yourself got lost in your efforts to please everyone around you and neglect who you were as a person. You try to be someone else to make others like you, to have others call on you in their time of need and disappear when you need them the most. It happens. In the process of trying so hard to have others like us, we lose ourselves. This chapter is here to help you to remember who you are. To remember how powerful you can be and to remember how worthy you are.

Time and time again, we lose ourselves in the fold of how society wants us to be and how they want us to react. We tend to forget who we are that we end up being someone who we do not recognize. But I am here to tell you that you get to find that person again. You get to love that person again and you get to have the life you have always wanted for yourself. It is easy to have others tell you who you are supposed to be, how you're supposed to act and what you're supposed to eat. Yet, we forget to love who we are as a person and what our unique self can bring to the table.

> Self-compassion is simply giving the same kindness to ourselves that we would give to others.
> – Christopher Germer
>
> TooMuchonHerPlate.com

You're probably wondering how self-care correlates to self-love or why self-care is important to practice. The answer is quite simple. In order to fully care and love another person, we have to learn how to love and care for ourselves first. I am a strong believer in self-love and self-care even though it took me a long time to get there. But even the littlest action that we take in self-care can go a long way in changing your view of yourself and others around you.

Everybody's way of self-care is a lot different than what your version of self-care is. Your version of self-care could be getting a massage, just taking the time out and taking a much-needed nap. By getting all the kinks out of your body, you can start to relax and just enjoy the rest of the day. It could be going on a hike, doing yoga or taking a kickboxing class. The options are endless when it comes to self-care.

My version of self-care does not have to be your version and it does not have to look the way that you envision your self-care. Below in our Question & Answer section, you get to write what your ideal self-care day would be. You get to practice that. You get to take one day out of your week - it could be a Saturday or a weekday and you get to do a day of self-care. You get to do that at least once a week. Do something that makes you happy, something that makes you jump out of bed and say, "*Yes! Today is my day! I get to take care of myself!*"

It doesn't matter what you have going on in your house. Yes, things get crazy. You could have kids that you have to take care of, but you get to have someone take care of them for you, while you tend to yourself. You can't give your children 100% of you all the time, while you give yourself 5%. By incorporating self-care into your day, you get to take care of your body, take care of who you are as a person, and be happy during that process. Below, I will show you how self-love can look like through the eyes of different people and different circumstances.

1) Taking 30 minutes for yourself to get ready for the day or to go to bed.
2) Taking a couple of hours to get a manicure and pedicure.
3) Have someone do your hair because you don't to have to deal with it yourself.
4) To wear clothes that make you feel good even if they aren't in fashion.
5) Reading a book that you enjoy by the window to get away from the stress around you.
6) To have candles surrounding you while you take a nice, long bubble bath.

7) Lastly, to take a nap and not worry about what goes on around you.

These are just some examples of how you can start practicing self-love. They can be an hour or more. It depends on how much time you want to dedicate to yourself that will make you happier. Life will always disrupt our day, but by taking time out of your day for you, you can be one step closer to being happier.

I personally dedicate Saturday for my self-love day. A lot of the time I go out for a date with my boyfriend on Saturday and the process of getting ready is my time to pick out the clothes that make me feel happy. If we do not go out, I take a couple of hours out of my day and get a mani/pedi.

By taking a few hours out of your day to do what makes you happy, the process helps to get your mind, body, and spirit ready for what is next to come. It doesn't have to take an entire day to get to the point of happiness; it is what you make your time out to be in order to be happy. This also helps you to learn to let go and also to forgive yourself. You are able to listen to yourself and sort out whatever it is that is causing an abundance of stress in your life.

"Care for your body and your body will care for you. Love your body and your body will love you too."
~ Mary Jelkovsky
Founder of Mary's Cup of Tea

As I mentioned above, you get to write out what your self-love day would look like. And then you get to practice that and take one day to do what makes you happy. What makes you happy could be going on a hike. What makes you happy could be going to the gym that you said that you would go to, but you haven't gotten around to yet. What makes you happy could be going to walk your dog at the park, letting him or her run around. Self-love could look like being out in nature and meditating, and really just taking the time out of your day and not worrying about what's going on around you.

So, I would like you to write out your ideal day, and then on your calendar put "Self-love Day" for the day you chose. By deliberately taking the time out to do it, you will be shocked and amazed at how great it will be to take that day and dedicate it to yourself. It's amazing what self-love can do for you.

Someone once told me that you are showing yourself love everyday by waking up, taking the time to get ready for the day, and taking care of your overall health. We are practicing self-love every day that we do not even realize we are practicing it. Routine is so ingrained in us that the care and love we show to ourselves just by going about our day has a totally different meaning to us. We think we have to take extra time out of our day to do self-care; in reality, we are practicing it from the moment we wake up to the moment we go to sleep. Even sleep is self-love. We are reenergizing our bodies for the next day and calming our minds.

Self-love is everywhere. All we need to do is take a pause from life, reset our intention for the day, and remember what we want to create in our lives. Loving yourself doesn't have to be a major production, just what makes us happy, makes us feel alive and—most importantly—what feels right for you.

Question & Answer

What is holding you back from loving who you really are? When did this feeling arise in you? Is it an external or internal force that is holding you back?

If you could add one thing to your daily routine that incorporates self-care, what would you add and how much time would you give yourself?

If you had one day to dedicate to self-love, what would it look like?

Chapter 4

Shifting the Mindset

"Self-love is the elixir of the immortal heart"
~ Amy Leigh Mercree, author and medical intuitive

Our lives are constantly changing and through that change, we are always shifting who we are to fit that change or circumstance. Yet, we forget to do that when we try on clothes or even when we choose to eat healthy. How do we go through everyday life so oblivious to ourselves that we care more about pleasing people instead of our own integrity? People fail to realize that you can do something about it. You can shift your mindset on how you interact with yourself and others around you. It is not something that is going to happen in an instant. It takes practice.

I have struggled with learning to stop caring about what others think about me. I thought that by making others happy, I was making myself happy. But deep down, I couldn't stand looking in the mirror because I didn't know who I was looking at. Through coaching and reading others' stories to self-love, I could learn to love myself. All because I shifted my mindset of who I was.

When I was single and dating, I wanted to be who other people wanted me to be. If they liked basketball, I liked basketball. If they complained that they were cold, I would try to warm them up even though I would be freezing myself. I lost who I was and started to end those relationships because they weren't what I wanted. I just went from one bad relationship of pretending to another. I ended up praying for a man to love me for me and not someone I was pretending to be. Once I shifted my perspective about relationships and set my intention, I opened the doors to the perfect man for me.

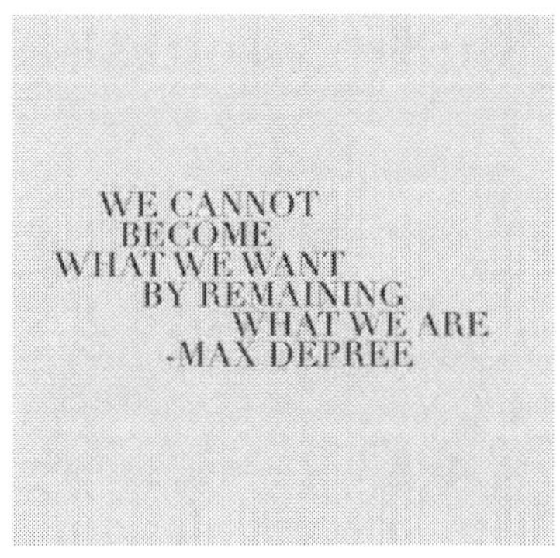

There are many instances in life that block us from making a shift for the better. Some examples can be in the form of negative thoughts we tell ourselves, negative feedback we receive from others around us, or how we feel in our own skin. Our bodies can tell us a lot about the way we are treating it. If your skin tends to breakout a lot, it could be a sign of stress or something is wrong with our digestive system. If you are overweight, it could be from eating the wrong foods that are harmful for your body or you could be depressed. I know a lot of people that are depressed and try to tell others around them that they are happy. When in fact, they are not happy at all on the inside and the way they deal with that stress is to binge eat. I know some people that are skinny and aren't happy. They think that for them to be happy they need to keep perfecting their bodies to a dream body.

People there is no dream body. You have one body and the way you choose to treat it will be displayed on the outside. It doesn't matter if you are skinny or fat. You are perfect the way you are and no one should tell you otherwise.

In order to be happy with yourself, your perspective on life and yourself need to be in aligned with one another. Below are some steps you can take to get there:

1) Seek new friends that uplift you.
2) Practice meditation.
3) Retrain your brain towards more positive thoughts (i.e. positive music).
4) Write out a 5-year plan.
5) Take a personal development class/training.
6) Do something nice for someone else.
7) Enjoy leisurely shopping.
8) Take time out for yourself.
9) Choose to be happy!

It doesn't take much for you to shift your mindset. You have to be willing to do so and to trust the process. It is all a process that will take as long as you are willing to put in it. Self-love is not something that will change by one thought.

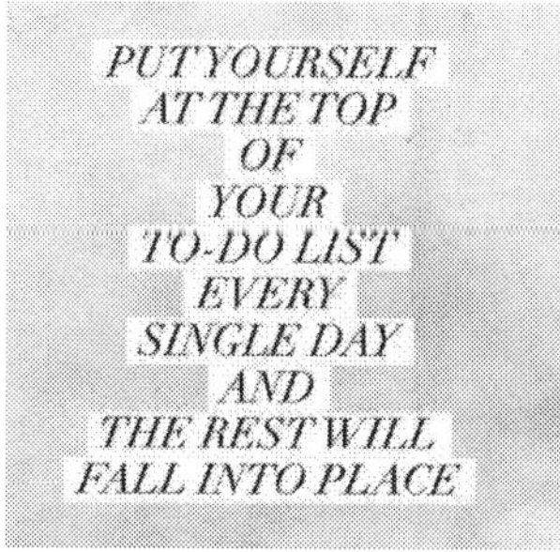

I have never had any fun shopping for clothes. My legs were too long for regular pants. Shirts that I tried on were meant for people with small arms and bigger chests, both of which I did not have. It took going into a store and trying on multiple styles of shirts to see what fit me. If it didn't make me feel good to have it on, then I did not buy it. I would get so depressed and vow never to shop again. However, I always needed clothes for work.

So, what are some things that you would like to change about your body? If you could somehow have a magic wand that could create miracles, what would you change? And why? If your "why" is because you don't feel pretty, let me just say that is B.S.! You are beautiful just the way you are. There is nothing that you need to change. If you are working out because you want to look skinnier or you want to fit into a size 2. Well, let me tell you, size 2 is hard to get into! I've tried. The last time I was a size 2, I was probably 14 years old. I haven't been a size 2 since. I'm not saying it to be mean or cruel, but that's not the ideal weight for me and not something that I look forward to being again. What you want to look forward to is loving yourself and loving your body the way it is.

The more you show love to your body, the more your body is going to change for you. **Your body changes according to your mindset.** Negativity produces a negative outcome; positivity produces a positive outcome. I have been negative about my looks and my body changed in a negative way. I grew in pant sizes and started to create holes in my pants by my thighs. Once I changed my mindset to positivity, my body started to change again. I started to lose weight and go down in my pant size. Your body feeds off your emotions and your mindset. If you are having trouble with your changes, journal or meditate. Journaling could look like just writing words that come up for you or feelings that you want to write down. It doesn't have to be many pages and could be just one word. Guided meditations have helped me to get in the practice of meditating and to start quieting my mind. Through introspection, you can find the root that is causing those issues and change the direction that tree is taking. Make it positive. Make it happy.

If you are having issues with your diet, start making changes towards it. Start by cooking your meals so you can know exactly what is going in your food. If you're like me and cannot easily create a meal, look up recipes of your favorite meals and start cooking them yourself. You can always tweak the recipe to make healthier or taste better. Setting aside time for to cook can seem hard, but if you create a schedule for yourself and say, "*From 6pm to 7pm I will be cooking dinner, or I will be cooking my lunch for tomorrow,*" you will be filling your body with the nutrition that it needs, rather than what is quick and easy. Yes, fast food is quick and easy, but does not do the body justice. And even salad from McDonald's—how do you know it's not manufactured in an area where there aren't pesticides? They can say anything they want in their advertising, but a lot of those advertisements are false and misleading. So, treat your body like you would want somebody to treat you. Treat your body with the love and respect that you would want someone to show to you.

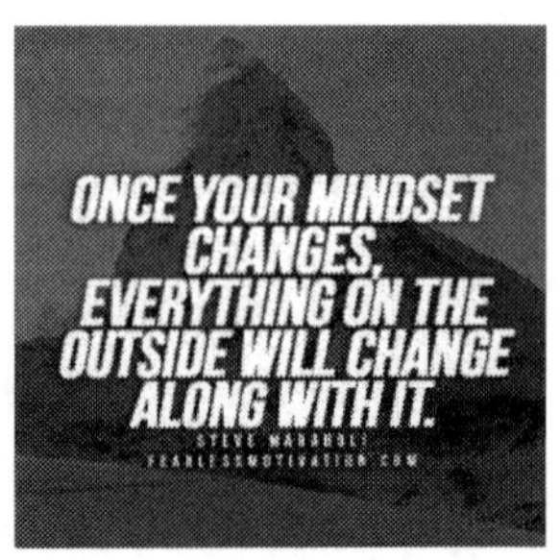

That is where the true challenge is and we get to shift that. We get to shift our mindset, to do the things that make us happy, and make our body happy. Being happy is a mindset that we get to create for ourselves. We do not need to be happy for others, but only for ourselves. We choose that and we practice that every day. We get to choose to be happy when life tries to get us down. Instead of letting it take over our happiness, we shift that energy to positivity. There are 86,400 seconds in a day. Letting something that ruined 10 seconds of your day should not reflect the other 86,390 seconds of your day. There is so much you can do in that time that will serve you for your day and intention that 10 seconds will amount to nothing but wasted space and time. Choose to be happy for yourself because you are special and deserve to be happy.

Shifting comes when somebody says, "*Hey, you're ugly,*" and you can reply, *"You know, I get where you're coming from, but that does not apply to me because I know how great I am as a person, and I am not going to stoop to your level. So, if you want to call me 'ugly,' call me ugly all you want, but I am not ugly. I see something in me that you do not see in you."* And that is being polite. That is telling people, *"You can throw words at me, but I will take those words, and I will shift it to where it does not have a negative impact on me."*

The more you are happy, the more others are going to be happy. Your attitude about whether you want to remain in the negative is where you get to change who you are as a person, what you want from society, and what you want from your peers around you. And if you are hanging out with a crew that is nothing but negative, this is where you get to shift your mindset of what a friend is compared to what it is you want from a friend. If you want somebody that uplifts you, you get to trim the fat by trimming people who are constantly negative from your life and bringing in people who are positive.

You get to be the person that you want to be out in the world, rather than what others want you to be. So, this is where we shift. We shift that mindset of, *"I look ugly. I can't do that"* to *"I look pretty. Let's give it a shot. Let's see if I can do it before I say no. Let's try it anyway, and see what magic can happen out of that."*

In the questions below, I want you to think about it. I want you to think about those negative conversations that we have with ourselves. Really capture what it is we would rather hear that is more positive for us to help create the change that we want in our lives rather than what's negative.

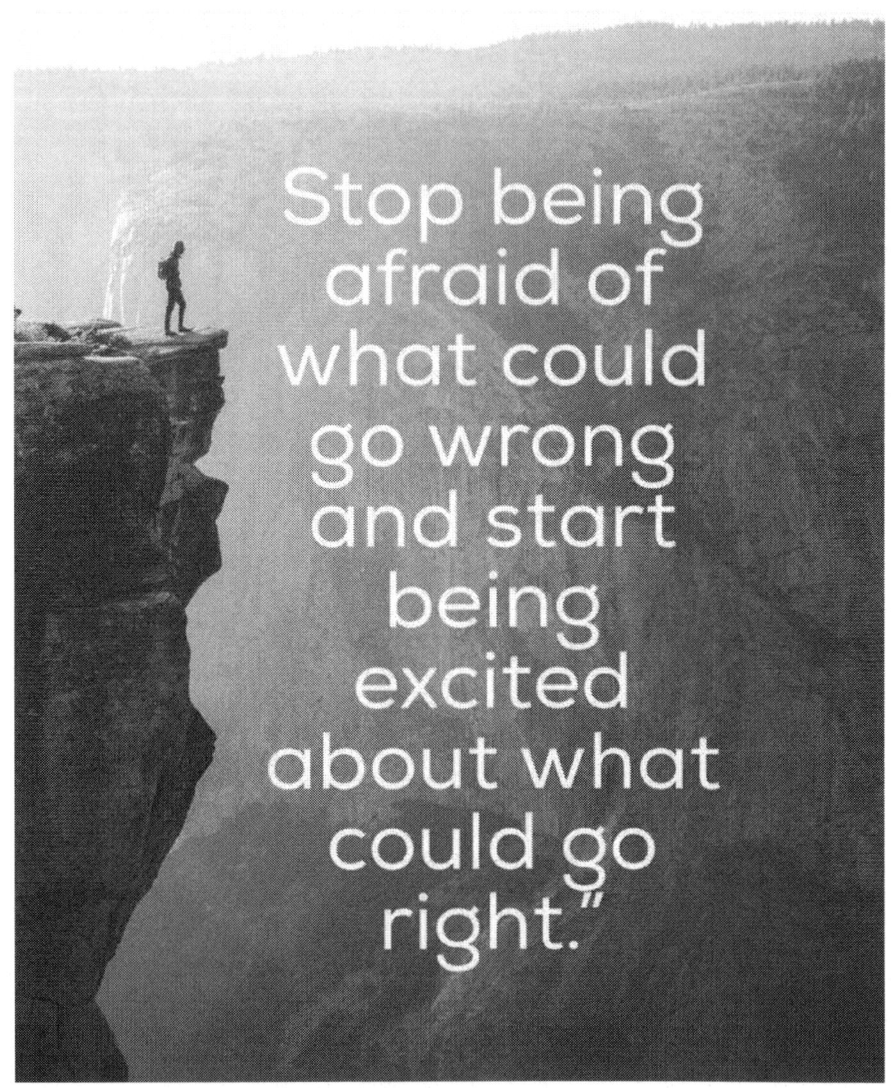
Stop being
afraid of
what could
go wrong
and start
being
excited
about what
could go
right."

Question & Answer

What are some negative conversations that you have around yourself?

How can you shift those negative conversations to be positive?

How would you feel being yourself rather than hiding who you truly are?

Chapter 5

Self-love Affirmations

"You only have one chance at this life of yours and you deserve to make it a great one." ~ Eva Medilek
www.thestylemogul4success.com

Self-love affirmations are needed to help us function in the world around us. We all need to feel loved. When we do not love ourselves, then we do not allow the space for others to love us. We all feel sad, rejected and hurt sometimes. We strive so much on the acceptance of others that when we are in a toxic relationship, we have a hard time getting out of it.

Friendships will come and go, but the true friends that can see deep within our souls stay with us longer. When the friendships go, we tend to think that it is because of something that we did or didn't do to keep the friendship going. We place the blame on ourselves and thus cause negative reactions.

When I felt that way, I tend to lock myself in my room and cry. The emotions that go through me are loss, anger, loneliness, sadness, and I feel as though no one cares about me. I keep my emotions bottled up because I am always afraid of what would come out of me if I opened up.

The thing is, it's okay to open up. You never know who can be there for you if you do not let anyone in. I used to always be there for my friends through the good and bad. When I would go through my own breakdowns, they were never there. Never answered my text messages or made an excuse that they were too busy. I thought that I was in the wrong and I would start feeling bad about asking them for help. So I stopped and bottled everything inside me until I was by myself.

Affirmations help us get through all the negative feelings that we have. They can lift us up high to help us get through our breakdowns. And they can help us live the life we want. Here are some photos below that help illustrate what affirmations can look like.

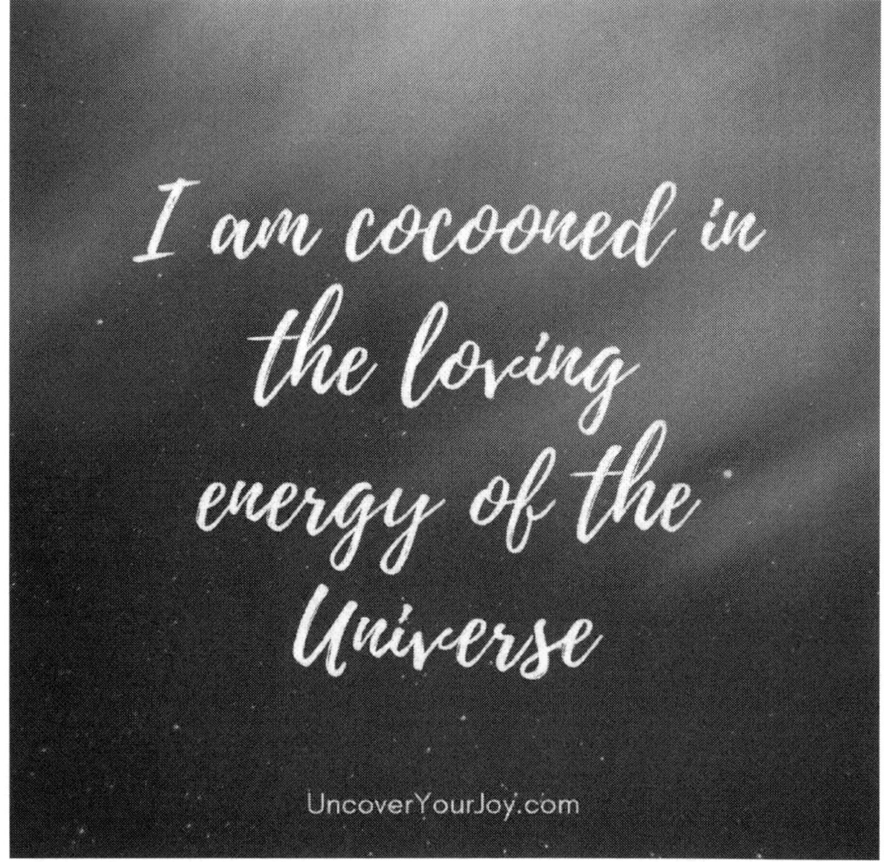

When we learn to listen to the universe and let its love wrap itself around us, we are able to let go of any inhibitions we may have and learn to let go. The universe is constantly trying to tell us what we refuse to hear. We stop listening to our gut feeling and wonder why nothing is working out like we want it to. But when we stop and listen, the universe helps to guide us where we want to be.

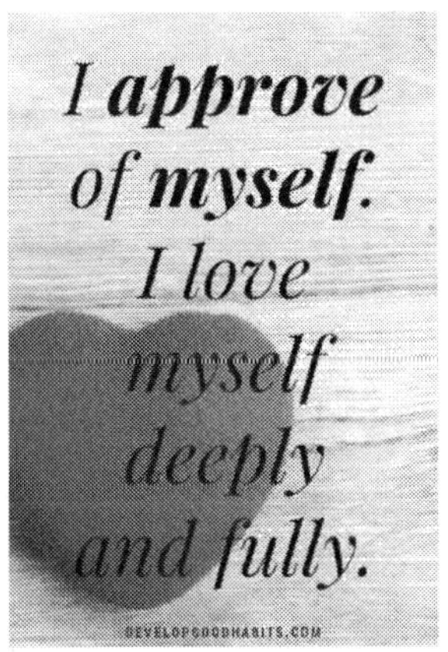

Love who you are. There is no greater affirmation that you can give to yourself than one of acceptance. Many people struggle with this to the point that the words do not hold any meaning to them. Approving yourself means accepting who you are and not for who you want to be. You are able to love yourself and not worry about what others think. Just saying the words "I love you" to yourself every time you look in the mirror can have a major impact on your outlook of yourself and your well-being.

*"POSITIVE
AFFIRMATIONS FOR
SELF LOVE:
I LOVE MYSELF UNCONDITIONALLY
I AM WORTH LOVING
I AM BEAUTIFUL
RIGHT NOW AT THIS VERY MOMENT I
ACCEPT MYSELF
I AM FREE TO EXPRESS MYSELF TO THE
WORLD
I CAN DO ANYTHING"*

You are worthy of everything around you. You are enough. You are beautiful. You are free to be yourself to those around you. You can do anything you want. The more we say those words to ourselves, the more we believe it. Do not let the negativity of others sway you to believing what they want you to believe. You are your own person and you have your own beliefs. Just because you don't align with other's beliefs doesn't mean you are not worthy. You are worthy in every way possible. Don't dim your light for others. Keep shining bright for you.

As I mentioned in one of my previous chapters, I have an older sibling that used to tell me that I wasn't pretty, that I wasn't smart, that I was adopted as I was growing up. It hit me at a time when I was most vulnerable and it stayed with me longer than it should have. But at the same time, I started to learn that I am pretty, I am smart, and I can do things. I do them in my own time and at my own pace, but I do them in the way that makes me happy. I'm not in a rush to do things because I know I have my whole life ahead of me. And whatever I do, I want to believe in it before I commit to it. We're constantly in a rush to complete things, to be ahead of the game, to get to the life that we want to live sooner rather than later. We rush to the end, and then when we get there, it's like, *"Now what? Now what are we going to do with our lives?"*

Again, this is where you get to shift. This is where you get to say, *"Yes, I am smart. I am happy. And things will come to me in life in it's own way and time."* One of the lessons that I learned from Jenna Phillips Ballard, *Founder of Unicorn University, Cofounder of Ascension Leadership Academy and Funder of I•▲M*™, was to live my life in abundance. To do that is part of self-affirmation, but it's also just reminding you that there is abundance in your life, whether it is small or big. The fact that you are alive means you are abundant in life. The fact that you are breathing means you are abundant in breath. It can be small things that add up to bigger things. The more you live your life in abundance, the more you realize that you may not be in a situation that you want to be in, but you are on your way.

It also requires patience. You're not going to get to the level of self-love where your self-affirmations are every day, back-to-back, no-hold-barred. There are going to be times when negativity creeps up on you. It will try to take a hold on your mind and keep playing the same words over and over and over again that you were working on releasing. You will learn to overcome those negative feelings, acknowledge them, and let them know they do not rule you. It will take patience with yourself and also to know that there is always a light at the end of the tunnel.

That patience will add up because it will get to the point where the negative thoughts that flow through you will just be background noise. You let it flow through you and you let it out. You can change those negative words by saying, "I am happy. I am in a place in my life where I can be free to be me. I don't have to rush. I don't have to do the things that everyone else does. I can be me and be happy being me." And that's where self-affirmation comes from.

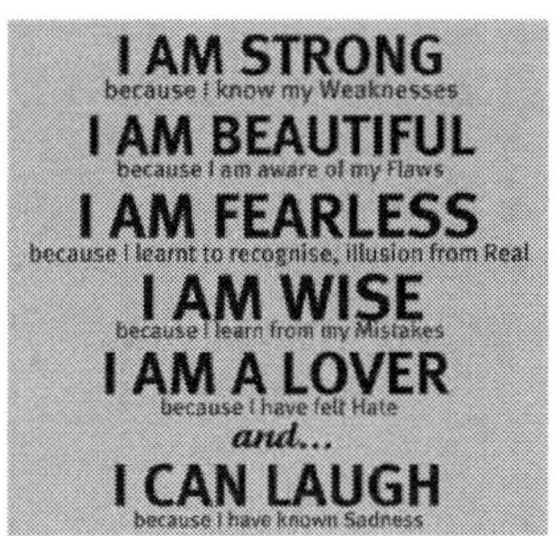

If you want to have a good day, listen to a good-day song. And that changes everything for you. It doesn't matter how much stress comes throughout the day because of work, you just know it's going to be a good day. A good day could be not cheating on your diet. A good day could be not eating that last piece of cake and saving it for tomorrow. A good day could be, *"Wow, I got up and I made it to work. And I didn't have an accident on my way to work."* That's all we need - just a little encouragement, because a little goes a long way.

So when you're thinking of how long something is going to take, there is no time limit on yourself. You can do things in your own time. Everything comes with practice, and like I said, practice makes perfect. With self-affirmations, it's a practice, and you can perfect it throughout the years, but there will come times when negativity creeps up on you and you get to shift. You only have one life and what your future will be depends on how you live it. Through self-affirmations - saying that you're smart, saying that you're beautiful - you can help shape your day. So, don't ever be afraid to be happy with who you are and what you bring to the table.

IT'S THE REPETITION OF AFFIRMATIONS THAT LEADS TO BELIEF. AND ONCE THAT BELIEF BECOMES A DEEP CONVICTION, THINGS BEGIN TO HAPPEN.

~ Claude M. Bristol

Question & Answer

Self-affirmations help us to grow and develop as a person. What are some ways that we can use self-affirmations in our everyday life?

____

____

____

____

____

____

If you could get rid of 1 negative thought, what would it be?

____

____

____

____

____

____

____

____

____

What are some ways we can combat negative feelings about ourselves with self-affirmations?

What would your day look like with positive thinking and affirmations?

Chapter 6

Embracing the Unique You

"As soon as you realize how incredibly unique you are, and own it, you will reach the the next level of self-love. And I say next level, because self-love is a lifetime journey.
You get to continue to love yourself day after day."
~Cole Bombino
Founder of the Freedom Project

This is one of my favorite chapters and one that I hope you all will enjoy. Embracing the unique you requires standing in your power, owning your voice, and being happy with who you are. Not trying to be like everyone else because that's just not the way life is. You can't go around being someone else when you're too afraid to be yourself.

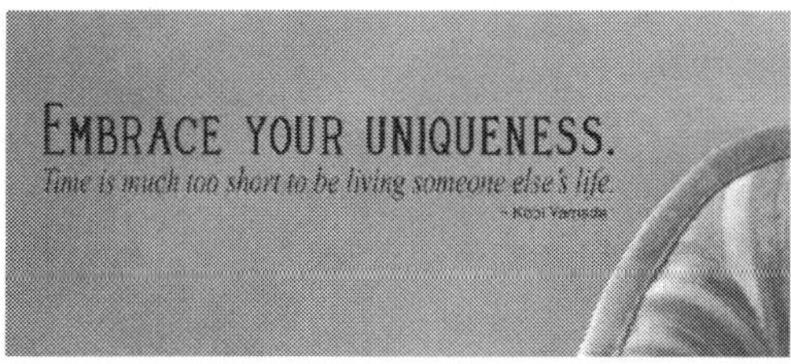

Embracing who you are is one of the most important things we can do. There is only one you, one genetic makeup of you, and there will never be another that is exactly like you. You should never be afraid to express yourself or be bold and loud.

For me, it took a lot of training, a lot of realizing my own power, and being able to be free to be myself. It was hard having all that power and just not knowing how to use it, how to shape it. I used to let everyone walk all over me. I used to let my mom walk all over me, my sister walk all over me, everyone in my family walk all over me, and even my friends and co-workers. And it got to the point that I just thought I was lost in sea of people because I felt as though my voice didn't matter.

Ascension Leadership Academy (ALA) helped me to get to the place that I wanted to be in my life and that I thought I could never reach. They opened my eyes to the possibilities that I could see myself living. But most importantly, it helped me to be free to be me. When I would go to the clubs, I would love and embrace the darkness because no one would see the way I danced or even see me. I was hiding who I was out of fear. Since ALA, I could dance in the light with everyone else around me. I wasn't scared to be myself and I was able to stop judging myself.

You get to have that chance in your life too. You don't necessarily have to go to all of the trainings that I went through, but you can do little things for yourself. Whatever makes you happy. If it means going riding a bike, being in nature, or going to the top of a hill and just looking out and saying, *"Wow, I made it this far! This is the best thing ever!"* Or, it could be taking a day for yourself and surrounding yourself with self-care that makes you happy. That is what makes you unique, how you take care of yourself, how you take care of others, how you take care of your emotions, how you live your life to where it makes you happy. So, don't be afraid to be bold, to be weird, to be different, to walk with no shoes if you want to. If that makes you happy, walk with no shoes, and nobody should judge you. If somebody does judge you, it's probably because they're jealous and they're too afraid to do it themselves.

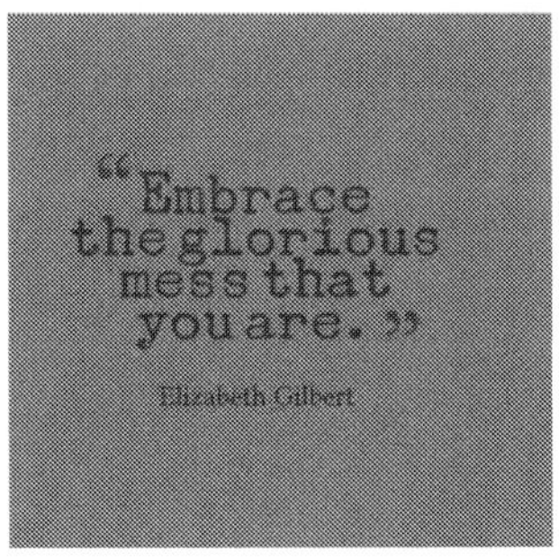

You get to be happy and you get to be bold, and there is nothing in your life that should hold you back from being you and being happy. You know, use that girlish charm of yours or that boyish charm of yours and be who you were when you were five. If you were happy at five, be that happy person. Be that happy girl. Be that happy boy. Be happy. And be you. Because the one thing we have in life is ourselves. No matter what happen,s all we have is us and our bodies.

What I've been saying throughout all of these chapters is that we only have one life, we only have one body, and the way we take care of it is the way we take care of others around us. So if we fill ourselves with negative emotions and bad food, then that's how we treat others; we treat others negatively. But if we take care of ourselves and if we put a lot of nutrients in our bodies, then we care about other people on the outside, as well. So it works both ways. And if you want to dye your hair purple, if you want to dye your hair green, if you want to dye your hair yellow, no one should hold you back from doing that. No one should hold you back from embracing the true you.

The true, authentic, vulnerable you is the one that everybody wants to see and the one that everybody gets to see because you are unique, you are beautiful, you are special. You are special to someone. There is someone out there who is going to love you for you and not judge you. They may say that you're crazy or a little weird, but then again, they're with you so they must be crazy, too! That's something I tell my boyfriend all the time. He calls me weird and I say, '*Well, you must be weird too, because you're with me. So two weird people think alike and they're meant to be together.*"

But that shouldn't sway you from being you. People want to see the authentic you because that is who they are going to love. And you should never be afraid to be yourself. You should never let other people's view of you dictate how you live your life. Embrace yourself. Embrace the unique you that makes you special because your parents, when they gave birth to you, saw something special and unique in you. It just takes you more time to realize that for yourself. And, yes, parents are always right, especially if you had great parents growing up. They're always right. It's just not easy for kids to tell their parents that they're right. Whether you had great parents growing up or had bad parents growing up, there was always someone there to help steer you in the right direction even if they played a small role in your life.

In order to be
Irreplaceable
one must always be
Different

—Coco Chanel—

It doesn't matter because eventually things start to click, things start to work, things start to come to life, because you are unique, you are special, and you can change the world for the better. People need to hear your voice and people need to know and see the power that you hold because you are strong, you are beautiful, you are confident and you are a star. There are billions of stars in the universe, and you are one of them. So be bold. Be happy. And remember who you were when you were five years old and how happy you were playing with your friends. That is the true you right there, and that's what you get to do every day. You get to do things that make you happy one day at a time.

Embrace your individuality. Love what you love without worrying about judgement.

AUTHOR EGYPT

Conclusion

Don't ever be afraid to love yourself. You are the only person in your life that deserves your love and attention. Your smile will brighten the whole room wherever you go.

The more we hide ourselves from those around us, the more we are denying them our voice. Practice self-love every day. And remember that you can do anything you set your mind to.

Be bold! Be brave! Be powerful! Don't try to be like everyone else. They cannot compare to who you are.

Love yourself and the world will follow!

30 Days to Self-Love

Day 1

This first week of journaling will be centered around meditation and getting in the mindset of self-love. The first meditation we will be doing is Self-esteem.
Learn to calm the mind and start to see what comes to you. Then write it down below.

Journal

<u>**Day 2**</u>

Today we will work on forgiveness. Write down what came to mind when you were meditating and who you were forgiving or letting go.

Journal

Day 3

In the next meditation, we will be doing will be a walking meditation. Whatever comes up for you during this meditation, please write below.

Journal

Day 4

Today, we will be meditating on the Relationship with Self. Journal your findings below.

Journal

Day 5

Today, we will be meditation on Relationship with Others. Journal below.

Journal

Day 6

We are almost at the finish line of meditation. The next meditation will be on Calming Anxiety. This will help with stress that comes up or negative feelings we are experiencing. Journal what comes up for you below.

Journal

Day 7

Lastly, we will be meditating on Happiness. What thoughts and emotions come up for you during this meditation. Can you feel yourself becoming happier?

Journal

Day 8

New week, new journal entries. For this week, we will be concentrating on ourselves. Today, you will be writing down 5 things that you love about yourself.

Journal

Day 9

Find an old picture of you and a family member. Write about the positive things they have done to help you forward your life.

Journal

Day 10

Write about what it is that terrifies you about yourself. Then, write about what are some things that make you happy about yourself.

Journal

Day 11

If you could go back in time and change one thing from your past, what would that be?

Journal

<u>**Day 12**</u>

We all have flaws we wish we could change on our bodies. What are some that you have? List them below. Next to that list, write something positive about them.

Journal

<u>**Day 13**</u>

Positive reinforcement is great to have for ourselves. If you could pick a family member to say something positive to, who would it be and what would you say? After you've written it down, let them know.

Journal

Day 14

To complete this week, what are some things we can do to make this world a better place?

Journal

Day 15

This week will be all about random acts of kindness. Being kind to others helps us to be kind to ourselves.

Today, we are going to pass out a dozen roses to strangers. There is no rhyme or reason to it. It is just for a nice gesture.

Journal below what came up for you and how it made you feel.

Journal

Day 16

The act of giving to another less fortunate than us can have a major impact in our hearts. So, find a homeless person and ask them what they need. Journal how you felt in that moment and how much of an impact you made on them.

Journal

Day 17

Today is all about volunteering. Find a place that you want to volunteer at or have stopped volunteering at and lend a hand. Write how you felt to volunteer there or to find a place to go.

Journal

Day 18

How does it feel to help someone out? Not for charity or money, but to do so out of the goodness of your heart.

Journal

Day 19

Stand in front of a busy door and hold the door open for people either coming or going. See how they react and journal how the experience made you feel.

Journal

Day 20

Today, you are going to write 10 thank-you cards to 10 people that you are close to and send it to them. Write your experience below.

Journal

Day 21

On our last day of random acts of kindness, you will be paying it forward. Pay the meal or coffee for the person behind you. It will help cause a ripple effect and could help someone who needs it.

Write about your experience below.

Journal

<u>Day 22</u>

This week will be all about self-care.

Today, you get to do something that makes you happy and makes you feel like yourself.

Write below what it was and how long you took to do it.

Journal

Day 23

Find a quiet place in your house or at a park and read a book you have been *waiting to read.*

Write below what the book is and how it made you feel to take time out of your day to read it.

Journal

Day 24

We all have days that stress us out. What are some of your stressors and how can you change the negative to positive?

Journal

<u>Day 25</u>

Take care of your body today. Go to the gym and exercise.

Write below how that made you feel and what you did.

Journal

Day 26

If you tend to go out a lot for your meals, stay home and cook for yourself. Or, if you do cook for yourself, try a new recipe.

Write down your experience below and how it made you feel.

Journal

Day 27

When was the last time you took a bath? If it has been a while, take one today. Light some candles, play some music, and just relax in the tub.

Write your experience below.

Journal

Day 28

Do something that is out of your comfort zone. If it's something that you've always wanted to do, do it.

Write what you did and your experience below.

Journal

Day 29

Look in the mirror and tell yourself the following:

"I love you"
"You are worthy"
"You are enough"

Repeat that 5 times. Write how that made you feel below.

Journal

Day 30

This last journal entry is a free-for-all. You can journal about anything you want. This is for your eyes only, so feel free to share whatever comes to mind.

Journal

Links to Trainings

For Ascension Leadership Academy:
https://alasandiego.com/

For Grace:
https://boldlyembodylife.com/

Made in the USA
Columbia, SC
21 July 2018